This book belongs to

Airplane

Boat

Dog

Frog

Ball

Bee

Panda

Giraffe

Duck

Fish

Cat

Car

Cow

Tree

Rabbit

Bird

Lion

Elephant

PUZZLE MAP

PUZZLE MAP

MATCH THE FIRST WORDS

Airplane

Ball

Rabbit

Frog

Bee

MATCH THE FIRST WORDS

Tree

Dog

Fish

Duck

Bird

In This Series

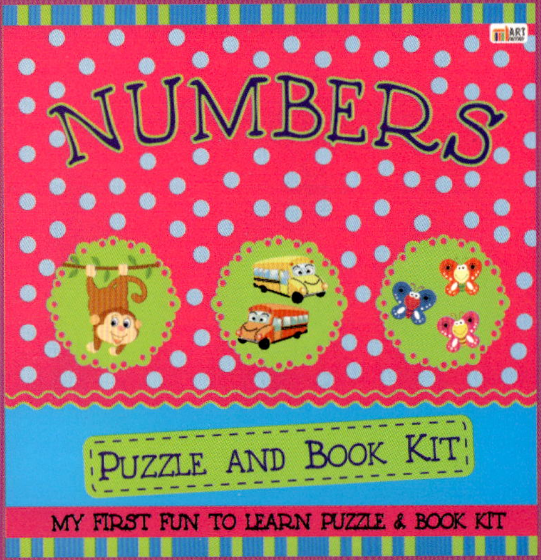

978-93-84227-12-8

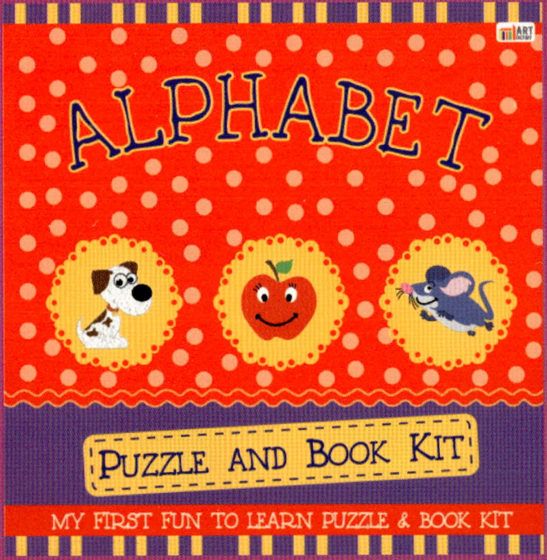

978-93-84227-10-4

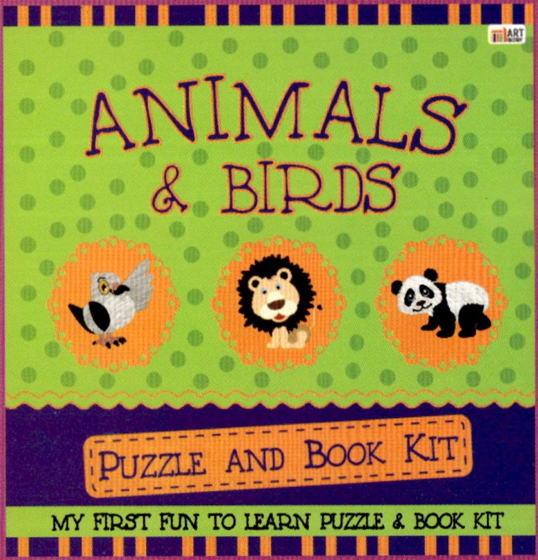

978-93-84227-14-2

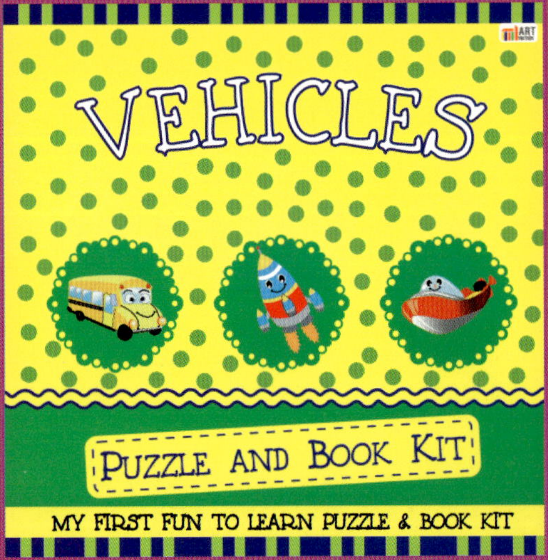

978-93-84227-11-1